# HOW I LOST 170 MILLION DOLLARS

My Time as #30 at Facebook

Noah Kagan

HOW I LOST 170 MILLION DOLLARS:
MY TIME AS #30 AT FACEBOOK
ISBN 978-1-6196130-0-3

http://AppSumo.com
http://OkDork.com

LIONCREST
PUBLISHING

www.lioncrest.com

Contents

Want more great stories, marketing tools, and business hacks?

》》》》→ OKDORK.COM/TACOS

You'll learn exactly how I started 2 multi-million dollar businesses, grew a 700,000+ email list, and where to find the best tacos in the world.

Introduction

June 16th, 2006 at 11 am was the moment I was fired from Facebook.

I remember that day vividly. It marked the end of one of the hardest working, most intense and amazing times in my life.

My manager, TS Ramakrishnan, asked me for coffee and to get updates on the latest projects, just like any other weekly check-in. I suggested a place nearby, but he insisted we go to another coffee shop on University Avenue in Palo Alto.

Entering the place, I immediately saw Matt Cohler sitting and "waiting" for me to arrive. I was a bit surprised. By the time I sat down, I knew what was going to happen.

You know that moment when someone says, "I have to tell you something," and they reveal something horrible, like they've been cheating on you? It was that same heart-stopping, body-chilling moment before Matt even started talking.

I blurted out instantly, "Am I getting let go?"

"Yes," Matt said.

My heart started racing. My mind couldn't believe this was happening. How could the "love of my life" and everything I've dedicated the past nine months to be over?

"This isn't real. It's a joke. Where are the candid cameras?" I was hoping to myself.

In the order that I ranked things in my life, they were as follows:

→ Facebook
→ Myself
→ Girlfriend
→ Family
→ Friends
→ Everything else

I was not alone with these priorities. Everyone else at the company was the same except the few who dated coworkers.

The rest of what we talked about sounded like a Charlie Brown skit. Blah blah blah blah.

I do recall asking if there's any way to save my job or what I could do to make it right. "Nothing," was the ultimate answer no matter from what angle I asked the question.

The meeting was over and so was my time at the company that was quickly becoming the hottest thing in Silicon Valley. Remember, this was when Myspace was still the hottest thing and Facebook was barely starting to escape being just a college social network.

We all walked back to the office. I was extremely embarrassed and wondered if everyone knew. I kept my head down. I had so much shame about myself. Everyone must be staring at me. Walking by my desk, Darian Shirazi, Facebook's first intern and now the CEO of Radius, asked "What's up?" He could tell something was off. I told him I got fired.

He was in shock. In the back of my head, I really wondered if any of the other engineers at Facebook were surprised. Maybe they had seen it coming. Maybe they had known. Some were glad, I'm sure.

I packed up my stuff, left my BlackBerry (remember those?), and left the building.

I felt like I had nothing. No job. I lived with six other Facebook guys, so no house now. No phone. I couldn't communicate with anyone. My world felt like it was crumbling.

Walking outside with nothing, they wouldn't let me take anything from my desk, I felt extremely empty. What the F could I even imagine doing next? My brain was racing at unprecedented speeds: revenge, guilt, regret and disbelief.

Seeing a Verizon store on University Avenue, I swerved into

the parking lot and told the guy behind the counter I was fired and if I could borrow a phone. He graciously obliged.

My first call was to my girlfriend, Jennifer. She was in disbelief and asked me what I was going to do. I told her I had no idea, but that I'd see her tonight. She was sweet and supportive as always, but I felt so embarrassed and in shock to share that news with her.

Then I went to the liquor store and bought a pack of Marlboro lights. I quit smoking, but this felt like one of those right moments.

I drove to the "Facebook" house and went out to the second floor balcony. I slowly took drags on the cigarette, trying to process everything that just went down in the past hour. Unreal.

After 30 minutes of praying I wouldn't see any of the other guys at the house, I packed all my things into my tiny two-door Honda del Sol. Fortunately, it wasn't much, but I knew that continuing to live with all Facebook people was not going to happen. My living situation was another casualty in addition to the majority of my social life.

My next stop was to my good friend Johnny's house. I was supposed to be at his house for a barbecue that night anyway, at which were a lot of Intel people with whom I used to work. When night came, they asked me about Facebook, since they used the site religiously and I had to lie and tell them that things were great. I couldn't bear to let the news out. You can't imagine how it felt to lie and tell them things were great. I had just had my worst day ever at Facebook, the company for which I left Intel.

I ended up drinking as much wine as I could and passing out on Johnny's couch that night.

The next day, I told my parents. I thought of how it must feel for them to tell the rest of the family about my failures. My mom was supportive and said to come home whenever I was ready. Good ol' reliable mom.

For months afterwards, I thought that everyone at Facebook must miss me. I thought that Monday when everyone returned to work and found out I wasn't there anymore would be a tough day for the Facebook employees...I got no well-wishes or hey, we're going to miss you notes from anyone at the company. That was part of our natural selection culture. The best survive. That's how the company got to accomplish "world domination" which was what Mark always wanted. I hoped more than anything they'd regret firing me and the website would come crashing down to a burning flame.

Over time, I realized how wrong that mindset was. Time goes on. People get back to work. And Facebook eventually became one of the most popular sites in the world.

Even that hope of them failing in the beginning didn't make the next six months any less painful. They were some of the lowest times in my life. Getting that job at Facebook was one of the best things to happen to me. I remember how validated

I felt finally getting a job I could brag to people about, unlike the sexy grey cubicle walls of Intel.

How could this have happened? One year, I was enjoying my extremely boring and cushy job at "Inhell" (aka Intel), and the next I found the love of my life with Facebook, soon to be cut short after nine months. Fired. Let Go. However you want to frame it, it is one of the worst feelings to ever experience.

This is the story of those nine months at Facebook, how I got there, how I persevered, and how I kept going forward when it felt like everything that mattered was taken away. I was one of the lucky few outside of the founding team's close inner circle to join the ranks only a year after the company was founded.

Over those nine months, I had a hand in creating some of the products you've probably used on Facebook: Status (all the updates you do), Pulse (hottest trends on Facebook), Mobile, and Pages. You'll read how those products were built and what the culture was like at the time. And you'll also see Mark Zuckerberg's (or "Zuck," as we called him) early leadership techniques.

The goal with this book is to share my story of failure and perseverance along with hearing about the actual insides of what is undoubtedly one of the most influential companies in consumer technology today. Even in the early days, one can see the well-publicized hacker ethos embodied in the phrase, "move fast and break things," in the way we did things. And you'll read about the parties. Oh, the parties.

Let's get started.

Life Before Facebook

How the hell did I end up playing with an Excel sheet as my full-time job? You could say I wasn't in heaven working at Intel.

Originally, I was verbally offered to work at Google pre them going public. "Thank God," I said to myself. I'm going to be working at one of the hottest companies today and become rich as f*ck. I thought about which color Ferrari I was going to be choosing. Green if they had it.

I made it through all their interview processes and was told I had a job with them. My life was near complete. Give me five more years with a wife and kids, and my Jewish mother and meemaw (grandmother) could brag gladly to all their friends at the gym or bridge club, respectively.

One day, I got a call from the Google recruiter who said, "Uh, actually...you aren't getting the job, best of luck!"

Every time I experience failure or go through a difficult

experience, my first reaction after sulking for a good day (it's great to embrace that) is to figure out what I can learn from that experience.

I reached out to Jonathan Rosenberg (now VP of Marketing) and Susan Wojicki (another big timer at Google). They couldn't legally give me feedback about what went wrong.

There was a silver lining from the experience. I got an invitation from Gmail when they were still in private access. Victory is mine!

Back to the drawing board...While at Berkeley, everyone in the undergraduate business school ended up at traditional jobs:

→ Accounting
→ Auditing
→ Consulting
→ Utility or Fortune 100 Companies
→ Banking

Pick your poison. NONE of those options sounded even remotely appealing. After the Google rejection, I wasn't super interested in job opportunities from Bank of America in North Carolina or at Philip Morris slanging cigarettes.

Fortunately, I still had Microsoft. I interned in Dallas, TX the summer before and accomplished my life goal of meeting Bill Gates at his house. It's almost guaranteed as long as you don't fuck up that if you intern somewhere you get the job when you graduate...I didn't. They didn't have any openings in the

Texas Sales & Marketing group I was with so I interviewed with the Xbox team.

The first question I was asked was, "Why do people play on a console over a PC?"

My answer: "Uh…I have no idea…ha ha ha."

Clearly, I hadn't played many video games in the past five years.

Luckily, my interview at Wells Fargo went well. I'd have to dress in khakis, button up shirt, and commute to San Francisco for a salary of $60,000 a year. My role, helping to manage and update their mid-tier client website. That sounded extremely unappealing. But hey, I appreciated getting an offer so I could, at least, have one option to fall back on.

The next company was Intel. How I heard about this job was almost as funny as getting it.

As a student senator at Berkeley, I helped a women's engineering group secure some funding. They subsequently added me to their mailing list. Email lists have always been good to me (my current company, AppSumo.com, is a mailing list for entrepreneurs)!

One day, as graduation loomed closer, Intel posted on that female mailing list that they were hiring two women for roles at the company. Fuck it. What do I have to lose I thought? Sent in my résumé! The name Noah could go both ways :)

Surprisingly, they called! WTF. Answered the phone and they rejected me for the female roles (obviously), but said they had a role in their Supply Chain Management team.

Sure, I'll interview. It's not a startup but it's a technology company and I could live in my parents' place in San Jose.

Walking into the huge complex it just felt like death. No colors on the walls. Every person I walked by had a blue employee badge and carried a sad face. Most seemed like their favorite things were waiting for 5 pm when they could leave, and weekends when they could avoid being at work.

I ALWAYS wanted to start my own company and ran many little businesses in college, but I expected to get a real job. It's what everyone was doing. Going against that, your peers, family, and expectations at that point seemed too daunting to me. Helps me appreciate people who do. So I figured I'd work at a big company to get experience, raise some capital, and then launch my own thing at night.

Unfortunately, that's not the case. At big companies, you get complacent, meet others who are like that, and end up learning the skills you need to work at big companies.

In retrospect, I would have focused on working at a company where I could have learned a lot from someone on the marketing team and really understood how to start a business.

During my interview at Intel, I distinctively remember talking with Torry who asked me where I wanted to be in five years.

I thought to myself and said, "Not here."

He took a minute.

SHIT, I shouldn't have been honest.

He BURST out laughing and said he felt the same way about leaving Intel (which he ended up doing within a few months).

Maybe there was some silver lining that came from working at this company with a few other young people who wanted to go and do something more exciting.

The rest of the interviews went fine. They were looking for someone who enjoyed technology and had a decent aptitude. Guess they had some low expectations :)

I got the job, a $60,000 salary, and my old room in my mom's house. A far cry from Google's lucrative stock options, which I'd already been daydreaming about.

My responsibility was to optimize the supply chain of Pentium 4 laptop chips. In theory, that sounds really amazing and a chance to learn how a company with $100 billion in revenues is run.

The reality was that I spent most of my time looking at an Excel chart that was manually processed while talking with our supply partners in the Philippines and Costa Rica. The rest of the time, I was on conference calls where I'd throw on a headset, hit the mute button, and chime in "Yes" every few minutes.

Intel was the place where parents with two kids, a mini-van and a mortgage spent the rest of their lives — not the place for someone hoping to start their own business.

On many days, I would bring my sleeping bag, strategically position it under my cubicle, block my door with a second chair, and get a good 2 – 3 hour nap. The rest of the time, I would take a two-hour lunch, work on my own businesses (a student discount card, Ninja Card; coordinate events called Entrepreneur27, and attempt to create a college Craigslist, CollegeUp) or go make out with my girlfriend who worked on the second floor. Hey, some nice perks of having so many conference rooms!

The best part of my job was with this master Excel sheet that I worked with. Everyone did it manually, but with macros and the solver function, you could automate a lot of repetitive tasks or guessing and checking numbers. So, I set that up after a month on the job and basically limited my actual amount of work to maybe one hour a day.

One of the amazing things about big companies is how the internal politics create an inertia of inefficiency. Everyone knew the Excel spreadsheet was not optimal, but we spent months in committees and meetings attempting to move it online and make it more efficient to see which production levels we should be targeting. It never happened in my one year and four months there. Hopefully, by now, 10 years later, they have it right.

The funny thing is I must have been doing something right; after a few months, I got a raise for my great performance! Or maybe that's just another sign of how inefficient the company is.

One of the biggest advantages of having a cushy day job was that it gave me a lot of time to work on my own projects. My mind had the freedom at night to work on whatever I wanted, and I had no risk if one of my side projects failed. To this day, I encourage people to not quit their day jobs until they have their side business going.

Another great lesson is to connect with other bright people. During my time at Intel, I put on mini-conferences and cocktail meetups. That put me in a great position for future jobs, meeting influential people like Blake Ross (founder of Firefox), my good friend, Ramit Sethi, of iwillteachyoutoberich.com, and Dave McClure (500 Startups), who kept me motivated.

In October 2005, I planned on quitting at the end of the year. Ha, I wanted to wait until I got my health insurance premiums. Yes, these are the excitements of working in a corporate life. I didn't know what I wanted to do, but I knew it wasn't going to happen while I was at Intel.

One day in October 2005, while wasting time as usual, I browsed Facebook in my cubicle. I browsed it so often that I noticed when a new "Jobs" link appeared in the footer.

Clicking that link would change my life.

The job was for a product manager. Never heard of that role or what exactly they did, but the description was about helping Facebook build more features.

I thought to myself, *this is the only other option I would even consider doing besides running my own business.* My father started his own copier business after coming to America and not being able to speak English. Following him into customer's businesses and seeing the freedom and control he had, showed me the type of lifestyle I wanted when I was working.

I knew the product was awesome, growing at a rapid pace, and didn't really expect to hear back if I submitted my résumé.

In retrospect, I suggest being referred to a company is the #1 way of getting hired versus just sending in your résumé like everyone else.

I knew the college market and building websites very well.

I'd been building things at Berkeley and at nights at Intel, such as ComeGetUsed.com (get it?), the largest book exchange on campus, and Ninja Card, a student discount card that expanded to five UC campuses and made $50,000 in its first year. And more things like that.

I didn't really want to work for anyone else, but submitted my résumé to Facebook anyway. I figured it was a long shot. Who actually looked at résumés submitted from the Jobs section? I wasn't expecting to hear back from anyone.

Surprise.

Two days later, I got a call from Sandy, the temp recruiter at Facebook. We talked about yoga, the college market, and my past work experience (in that order). Five minutes into the call, I was scheduled to come into the office to interview that week.

This still won't pan out, I mean, no one gets a job this way. Right?

I didn't know what to expect interviewing with a company where most people assumed Mark Zuckerberg and Dustin Moskovitz were the only employees. So I figured I'd talk about what I liked and disliked with Facebook, and in preparation, I made some mockups of features/changes I'd like to see on the site (making things more local with businesses) and a portfolio of all the projects I had created.

After all, I had to have some good ideas for Facebook. If working on a college student website like Facebook wasn't for me, I didn't know what other kinds of companies would be a better fit.

The Interview

I showed up for the interview during my lunch break at the Facebook office on University Avenue in Palo Alto, CA. This area is extremely famous and expensive. The top technology companies of the past 10 years all have had or had offices there: Yahoo, Google, PayPal and more. And it's just a few blocks from the gorgeous Stanford campus.

Taking the elevator up to the third floor, I had no idea what to expect besides this boy wonder from Harvard who created this site and maybe a few other people helping him work on it.

It was, as expected, a mess.

Upon entering, the office was a hybrid of fraternity house and office. Wooden Ikea desks were spread wherever they could fit in, cables were falling from the ceiling providing power outlets to all the computers, and everyone was on the latest MacBooks and huge monitors. This is at a time when Mac was still struggling and most people were on Windows laptops.

There were dozens of people all spread across the room, working in a very open environment. Most people glanced up from their monitors and just went back to work without even looking at me. The whole scene reminded me of a startup being run out of a frat house.

This was my kind of place. Come on! Compared to Intel, there were young people everywhere, a refrigerator stocked with unlimited Red Bull and everyone was working on a project they truly loved and used daily. *What more could I ask for?*

I wasn't super nervous going to the interview as I already planned on doing my own thing if I didn't get it. Don't get me wrong — I was very excited to possibly work on a site that all my friends were using daily but if I got rejected I already had a back-up plan.

The interview was easier than I expected. I later realized it was probably designed to see if I was a cultural fit more so than just intelligence. I was asked why I wanted to work at Facebook, how I would improve some new ideas they were working on (products like providing local business information to students which never ended up being released), and what features I wanted to see on the site.

I preferred this kind of interview to the Google-style questions: "How many toilets are there in the United States?" How many are there??? What does that have to do with anything I'd do at the job?

The Facebook people seemed so busy with the website that

the interview was more a verification that I "got" Facebook and had the aptitude to be managing new features for the website.

Questions included my previous employment, and what I did for fun. I interviewed with Ezra Callahan who was the company utility player, Dustin Moskovitz who was one of the five co-founders of the website, and Doug Hirsch who was the VP of Production and an early Yahoo! employee.

A few fun facts I shared/learned during the interview process.

While doing my HFG Consulting business, I worked for Dell who wanted campus representatives across the USA and Facebook allowed you to find and message anyone at that time, so I suggested they limit that.

Second, many of the top people in the company were poached from Yahoo! at that time, as well as recent graduates from Stanford and Harvard almost exclusively. There were a few who were not, but most people, including customer support, were Ivy Leaguers.

Dustin, who was then the CTO of the company, had never programmed before. He wanted to be a part of Facebook so he taught himself to code to work at the company.

Lastly, there were four founders after Mark who were the core of the company: Eduardo Saverin who we've all read about as he got pushed out of the company and recently got tons of Facebook shares for it; Chris Hughes who's now the editor of *The Atlantic*; Dustin Moskovitz, who now runs Asana, a to-do list company; and Andrew McCollum who is now an entrepreneur in residence (EIR).

The last person who was critical to the company was Adam DeAngelo, Mark's childhood friend. This guy is pure genius and very socially awkward, similar to Mark. They are shy, introverted and spend a lot of time thinking by themselves.

That was the core group of people who really put the site together and got it to the million-user level. And subsequently have each amassed huge amounts of wealth.

That day of interviews felt surreal. Could I actually end up working on the site I was playing with every day? I could message and poke any girl I wanted to and the clout I could use at nearly any bar I walked in to. The power seemed attainable and quite fun! (Hey, I was immature and greedy.)

This was vindication against Google; fuck them and their arrogant ways, rejecting me for a job. I was worthy, I was smart, and I am capable of doing great things, even if you said I wasn't. Okay, this sounds bitter and I was bitter. As I've matured, I've realized you have to decide your own self-worth versus letting others determine it.

Within just two weeks, I had three total rounds of interviews, received an offer, and became #30 employee at Facebook. The whole interview was a bit anti-climactic. Luckily, my résumé got noticed, I had some fun chats about which future Facebook features I could create, and soon enough, we were discussing my offer package. I was elated to be leaving Intel for what was, in my eyes, one of the hottest companies on the planet.

I was a bit surprised by the size of the company and to not have interviewed with Mark Zuckerberg. It kept me nervous about finally meeting him now that I'd be working at his company.

What I couldn't have imagined was becoming real. Pinch me. Okay, don't cause that'd hurt, but I couldn't believe it was becoming real, and I'd get to work in that chaotic mess of an office with amazingly bright people on a product that was shifting the world.

They offered me $65,000 and .05% stock of the company or $60,000 and .1% (20,000 shares at that time). At this time, it was as much as Intel, which surprised myself since you expected startups not to be able to pay as much as big companies.

To me, I knew the company would be a big hit and asked if I could even take less salary and more equity. They said "no" and so I officially on paper owned .1% of Facebook.

At today's market rate (3/20/14) that'd be worth around $170,000,000.

At that time, Facebook was growing by 50,000 people a day just in colleges. Everyone I knew used it and, personally, I thought relationships were the most valuable thing in life and Facebook was becoming the backbone for managing them.

Mind you, though, at that time, Myspace was significantly larger but I personally preferred using Facebook. More on that battle to come later...

I was living pretty cheaply at the time. My mom made dinner most nights or I ate tuna with frozen vegetables (surprisingly yummy) and didn't have student loans to worry about. So, the opportunity for less cash, and the upside, if the company went public would be large. I never expected it to get as big as it has become.

I was in denial that I could get paid to work at Facebook. That's like telling a college student they can get paid for drinking beer and partying, which, in retrospect, may not have been too far from the truth.

I was only 24. In my mind, early employees in those days made millions and retired at 28. The future seemed exceptionally promising and I hadn't even started working yet...

My First Day: October 2005

Two weeks later was my first day.

The building itself was unmarked, and the door was unlocked. Only a paper sign was taped in the window of the office. The place was a mess and pizza boxes were everywhere.

It didn't matter. I was in bliss. I was getting a chance to work on the hottest product in the Valley at the time.

I took up that same elevator with a ton of jitters and excitement about what I'd get to work on and my future.

On arriving, Dana, the other recruiter, handed me a laptop, welcomed me to Facebook and said to sit wherever I felt liked. Ha, what a drastic difference this was than the welcome package, online sexual harassment training, and meetings that welcomed me to my first day at Intel.

Stumbling over the cables and pizza boxes, I found the first person I recognized from my interviews, Ezra Callahan (now an hotelier in Palm Springs), and sat down at the Stanford graduate's desk. As I set up my new Apple PowerBook G4 laptop, my new boss, Doug Hirsch, hurried by and reminded me that we had a meeting at 1 pm. I had a few hours to get acquainted.

I had no idea what the fuck was going on. What should I be doing? I wanted to get right to work and feel valuable but where to even begin? I stumbled around on the laptop using the latest MacBook for the first time and waited for my next instructions.

Thirty minutes later, Hirsch walked by me and out the door. Over his shoulder, he said he'd see me after lunch. I was then immediately called into a meeting with Ezra and some other employees who I hadn't yet met. It was very quiet in this tiny office, and the tension was high. This was because Mark wanted to meet with us.

This was my first encounter with him; it was like seeing a celebrity at that time. I'd only read the online reports and magazine articles about this guy who started this website in his dorm room. Little did I know that I'd be at the center of the upcoming discussion.

Then he appeared. Mark walked in and everybody went silent. He looked flustered — a surprise, given that all I had seen by this point was his awkward, happy grin on TV and all over the Internet. But here he was, boy genius, *wunderkind*, in the flesh.

In my mind my heart was racing, it's him. He seemed about

the right height but more nerdy than I was expecting. It reminded me of when I was around Bill Gates. Awkward, very methodical in his speaking (he didn't talk right away), and spoke with a precision and brilliance that I hardly experience to this day.

My immediate feeling I had then and throughout my time there was a feeling of caution about what to say. I wanted to be smart; I didn't want to embarrass myself. I wanted to fit in without looking stupid.

He looks at me.

"Who are you?"

"Noah," I said. "It's my first day."

"Noah — got it. Uh, I just fired your boss Doug," he explains.

It's my first day and my boss gets fired? Shit, am I next? Only one hour in the day, FML.

So to appear witty and get on Mark's good side right away, I said:

"How do I avoid messing up so I don't get fired, too?" I said. Everyone laughed, but I was serious.

"Don't try to sell my company out from under me," he answered.

As a little background, Terry Semel of Yahoo! had been

negotiating to buy Facebook for $1 billion, which my now former boss urged Mark to accept. But Mark made it clear that that wasn't happening anytime soon. Whenever asked, he publicly stated, a line he firmly believed, "Facebook is being built for long-term success. Just like Google." That firing was a very clear lesson that it was Mark's company and he got to do what he wanted to do with it. He fired Doug immediately when he found Doug trying to get the deal to go through behind his back.

Mark later did a company meeting sharing the potential deal, and he explained that he'd never ever go along with. Ironically, now Facebook is worth four times more than Yahoo! Mark could have been wealthier than he could've ever imagined, but him stating he's not interested and showing it with the Yahoo! deal made it very clear to us how serious he was about Facebook for the long-term.

Mark finished our meeting by saying he would figure out how things would be structured, and that I should report to him for the time being.

"Oh," he said, with a small smirk, "And welcome to Facebook."

The Beginning at Facebook

My first night on the job made me realize I was working with people much smarter than myself and quite accomplished. Aaron Sittig, one of Mark's most trusted employees and lead designer at Facebook for years, had already helped create the infamous Napster. Most of the guys were the types who were picked on in high school, but were exceptionally gifted and went on to top schools (MIT, Stanford, CMU, or Harvard).

I was the only Berkeley guy. This put an inferiority complex in my mind that never went away. I always felt like I wouldn't be good, and for the next months, worked my ass off just to be looked at as an equal. It didn't help that many of them also carried over their Ivy League style of entitlement. As they talked, it was like things were guaranteed; it was a pretentious attitude that they and Facebook itself were destined for greatness.

My father came to this country with no money and sold carpets to make money; I wasn't raised with elite boarding schools like Zuckerberg. I was raised to be humble and work my ass off like my dad did. That felt more like my super power versus just the straight mental aptitude these people felt.

One day a month later, I joked to Ezra that we should hire more "stupid" people to be able to understand our users better. His response, which blew me away, was that we should hire even smarter people to really understand what the users really wanted. Another example of a common feeling I would have at Facebook, getting out-thought and not feeling good enough to be there.

Dinner on my first night was at Zao Noodles on University Avenue in Palo Alto with CTO Dustin Moskovitz (a Jew fro, pot smoking guy who had a mild arrogance about himself, his niceness to you was in direct correlation to how useful you were to the company), product manager Ezra Callahan (a Stanford graduate who was super smart and the only person to do every role in the company), Charlie Cheever (coding genius who always had a great attitude), Adam DeAngelo (super coding genius who was exceptionally quiet), and some of the original engineers like James Pereira (an awkward developer who worked part time in a movie theatre) and Karel Baloun (the grandpa of the group who had kids and was only in his thirties).

This group of people didn't feel like the friends I would choose to hang out with outside of work. They were smarter than my current friends which intimidated me, and only now in retrospect, helped me grow so much further than I could ever imagine. The one thing we all had in common was a deep love and commitment to Facebook.

From that dinner and the subsequent days, I made an effort to get to know every person in the company, including support staff (most of whom had master's or PhD degrees and were generally looked at as second class citizens along with us product managers), office managers, sales & marketing (mostly Naomi and Mark's sister, Randi), and anyone else who was around. I wanted to be accepted, so think of it like your first few days of a new school. That's what it was like.

Most of the people were already together from college or spent a fair amount of time outside of the office. I "tried" to be funny, asked people what I could help with, and went to any outing that was available to fit in. Those days, even if I didn't have work to do, I would stay as late as everyone else just to be a part of it.

Even from the early days, there was an electricity that we all felt and knew we were a part of something special.

I crossed paths with many people who'd go on to shape Facebook and startups in general.

Facebook, at that point in time, had the smartest people I've ever worked with. I never became very close with anyone there, but I can say this group of people amazed me and I grew the most professionally during that time period.

My First LIVE Feature

Even in 2005, Facebook existed on a large scale, with nearly 10 million people. Any feature, however minute, would be seen by millions of people. That was one of the things I took for granted when I was there.

Almost 50,000 people were joining a day. I couldn't even imagine that many real people in the world doing the same thing every day.

During the first week, I put up something live that hundreds of thousands if not millions of people were going to see instantly. If you've ever started your own site, you definitely take for granted the scale Facebook had and was going to have.

I vividly remember the first product I shipped. It originated with a brief direction from Mark.

"Noah," he mentioned offhand one day, "we need to add location to the photo albums. Go do it."

I couldn't contain myself. Mark had given me my first real assignment.

What the hell do I go do next?

There was no process for how things got built at Facebook. There wasn't a formal onboarding program like most major tech companies do for new employees today.

It was basically go find someone at a computer who can program but doesn't look busy, and see if you can convince them to work on your feature.

I've always built crappy looking websites where there wasn't much thought or discussion about features. More or less, I had an idea and let the developers I worked with make the decisions on those points.

It may seem trivial to add locations to a folder, but once you start working with developers you learn about EDGE CASES. They became one of the most annoying things about working at Facebook.

I grabbed Nico (the nearest developer) and thought it'd be easy to just direct him to add a box to the place where people were creating their photo albums.

But then he started asking me questions:

"What if they don't want to show the location to all friends?"

"What happens if they don't want to add location?"

"Do we enable type-ahead for the location?"

"Are we planning on using the location in other places in the future?"

Shit. Maybe I am way in over my head. Over time I learned our roles were to understand the flow of a product, help prioritize which products we would build, and oversee the QA (quality assurance) to get bugs fixed as quickly as possible.

I came back answering those questions, realizing most of them didn't matter, and Nico was quick to turn on the feature and promote live to the main site. That whole process was within an hour. Damn, this place moves way the fuck quicker than Intel. My kind of pace!

We triple-checked our work and then had Mark see it. He was the gatekeeper and god of all things Facebook. He approved and shortly millions of people were then interacting with something I helped create. POWER is mine :)

Once features were, live many of the students would let us know about bugs and that was how we could push things out faster and fix them quickly. Overtime, we'd integrate the support team to look for bugs in features before we released new features publicly. As always, the final say on almost all major releases had to go through Mark first.

Typical Day

Quickly, I established a daily routine at Facebook. It couldn't have been more opposite than life at Intel. And I loved it!

My day regularly looked like this:

9:30 am: Woke up hung over. Normally, the night before was a late night of partying at the Facebook house where I lived with six co-workers. One of the guys rented a huge two-story house in Palo Alto just 1.5 miles away from the house. No one wanted to live too far away. I wanted to get out of my mom's house and they had a spare room. These guys had all worked at Microsoft and went to Harvard together. They were friendly and accepted me, except Boz who was standoff-ish to almost all people. I recall most nights I'd stay up late intoxicated after work, discussing Facebook with the other guys and then stumble to my room and finish the night watching the show 24. Damn that show is addictive.

10:00 am: Headed into the office. I was one of the earlier ones in the office and started getting my day organized. I'd be there to see most of the engineers about an hour later. This was a nice quieter time to be in the office.

11:15 am: Checked emails and blogs like TechCrunch and Mashable to see what they were saying about us and what competitor had cropped up that day. Remember, Facebook wasn't the international behemoth it is today. Myspace was larger, Bebo and Hi5 were growing quickly, and new "social networks" were launching daily. I'd then go chat with other "early-risers" about their projects, figure out which projects were doing well and which weren't.

12:00 pm: Grabbed a delicious, catered lunch. These meals were amazing with a full salad bar, a daily variety of foods ranging from Vietnamese, gourmet sandwiches, premium drinks of any sort we requested, and any other type of lunch food you can imagine. In case you were wondering, I did gain about 15 pounds working at Facebook.

12:45 pm: Planned out new features based on directions from meetings with Mark on what he envisioned. The product managers would take notes in these meetings and finalize what needed to be done. Made sure the engineers were working on the right things. Working on the right things felt like helping do all the bitch-work engineers didn't want to do, like documentation for the help pages, testing the new products out, and coordinating larger projects across multiple engineers.

I used to joke to myself that my main job was to give them massages and help remove anything that would be in their way. Most traditional companies I learned, like Intuit or larger tech companies, had product managers make nearly ALL the decisions about features on the site. At Facebook, the engineers were insanely great and could make many of those decisions themselves. It proved truly difficult to figure out where I could be valuable within the company.

As we developed features, there definitely developed rivalries to impress Mark. It was a healthy competition that pushed everyone to keep working harder. This manifested from Mark generally favoring certain employees, and like a child, wanting to get that same attention from the "father." This manifested mostly from Mark being selective with praise and the type of Alpha people that were being hired at the company. We all wanted to work harder and create features that would make the site grow even larger. I was not a favorite.

2:00 pm: Partner meetings. We'd have daily conversations with potential partners. One day I got to meet Chad Hurley of YouTube before the site had taken off. He was really friendly and wanted to figure out a way that we'd promote their service within the fast growing Facebook. (Cool side note, Steve Chen, the other founder of YouTube, was an early Facebook employee who quit to start the video website.) For most of these meetings: a) I was excited to check out new companies; and b) no one else wanted to do them so I volunteered myself.

One particular meeting was memorable. Jeff Rothschild (founder of Veritas, which sold for hundreds of millions to Symantec, and general badass "old guy" at the company) and I met with Moo.com. They create unique and fun business cards. Jeff pretty much dismissed them and walked away from the meeting after five minutes. I stayed with Richard from Moo and had a nice conversation with him. We are still friends 10 years later. Jeff later that day remarked, "Why do we care about a paper company." Ha! We had blinders that everything NOT-Facebook was basically insignificant. That attitude of arrogance never really fit well with my style, but it was easy with our growth to start thinking that way.

3:30 pm: Worked with Customer Support (CS) team on common bugs they were hearing about and discussed new projects. The CS team was our group of beta testers that tested any new features we built before we launched them. Generally, we'd talk with Tom LeNoble or Paul Janzer, the CS leads, and their team about what could be better and faster before pushing them live.

5:00 pm: Checked email and tested new beta features. Many times, I would go to the different developers and see what they were working on during this time and what they needed help with.

7:00 pm: Catered dinner (woot). Hung around with the guys in the lounge area and discussed life. When we weren't working on the site, we were talking about the site. That consumed our life. We'd also start sipping on beers or the Red Bulls that stocked our fridges. Occasionally, we'd discuss the girls we were meeting through the site or the future demise of Myspace that we were aiming for.

8:00 pm: I researched new product ideas looking at sites like Myspace, Plaxo, and other international social networks, and thinking about how we wanted the experience to be ourselves, and drawing and writing out how that should flow. Discussions with Mark, Dustin, or others about how new features should work. This was a good time to have these conversations with Mark and Dustin, as they would typically stay there until 10 pm or later. They both intentionally lived within close walking distance of the office.

Facebook hardly reacted to what other sites did. We created the features and things we wanted, not what the users wanted.

Mark's major directive was everything for growth, or in his exact words, "world domination." The companies we all admired had either a great design or were Google/Apple who had super smart people and were outputting products we were using ourselves.

10:00 pm: Did some coding for bug fixes, help pages, and various parts of the site. Reviewed status on projects to ensure there were no speed bumps in the way.

12:00 am: Went home to party...

Why We Loved Being at the Office as Much as Possible

The boundaries between night, early morning, and morning were frequently blurred. Red Bull's Energy drink became our drug of choice, God bless those stocked refrigerators and our office managers.

The office really was a fraternity. Our original office was emblazoned with the Greek letters, Tau Beta Phi, AKA "The Face Book," and was covered with graffiti made by David Chiu who made millions since his work was paid with Facebook stock. There was actually graffiti of a woman shitting in the women's bathroom. It had to be removed as the company was hiring more female employees while it had been only guys till around employee #15, Naomi Gleit.

There was a patio on the roof where we would drink beers, smoke, and just talk about our future. For a while, unsurprisingly, people actually called the office "The Frat House."

The house doubled as the unofficial party house. It was here that I first learned about flip-cup, and lost numerous games. It was the home to Facebook debauchery whenever we weren't at the office.

Work never left us. Even when we would be crowded into someone's room, smoking weed and drinking beer, we'd be discussing the features and our ongoing work at Facebook.

It was like we were all in love with the same girl and there was enough to share. I know what you're thinking pervert, not like that. It was a shared purpose that we all felt valuable and meaningful, like being a part of the best team ever.

Even in that house I felt like I had to impress the other guys and show that I wasn't stupid or an imposter; that I could match their Ivy League wits. This was one of my ongoing struggles while working at Facebook though, not just in that house.

A party at our Facebook house was tons of good liquor, beer, a big house, and all dudes. It was the same as college, except with slightly older people. Imagine living in college but having the budget of your parents.

There was a standing poker game on Wednesdays. Creatively called "Poker Wednesdays," it was really just another excuse to party after work. Facebook generously catered these events with crates of Hefeweizen, and piles of pretzels, popcorn, chips, guacamole, and salsa. The buy-in was a mere $10 and was a great chance to bond with the guys.

I used to love these nights. We were loose from the beer and everybody would chat freely. It brought out everyone's more natural skills and personalities. Andrew "Boz" Bosworth (who came to FB with a foursome of other Microsoft/Harvard guys) was the poker professional who loved taking all our money. In addition, he talked a massive amount of shit, it got on all our nerves. The Colombian poker master and expert designer, Soleio, was the best at bluffing and a very smooth player. Dustin Moskovitz was a great player. I was always nervous to beat him for fear of losing my job.

Not really, but you always knew in the back of your head that he or Mark had that power. He never truly treated us that way but there was a confidence that he exuded.

One night, while waiting to meet with Mark, Peter Thiel (PayPal co-founder and early Facebook investor) bought in for $20. We were in the middle of a tournament, but he bought in anyway. After 10 minutes, Mark appeared and Peter stood up to leave for their meeting. He asked for his money back.

Hold on, we are all thinking to ourselves, *this billionaire is asking the kids who are making his equity more valuable for $20 back in a winner take all tournament.*

Fortunately, we had Boz in the group.

Boz simply said, "Go fuck yourself."

Ha, we all laughed. Peter bowed gracefully and walked away without taking any of his money.

I was a bit surprised but glad that Boz could be very direct.

Later that night, I busted out. As I was walking to my car being a poor loser, I saw Peter's McLaren SLR parked out front. It's a car that costs almost $500,000.

Go figure.

I Always Love to Root for the Underdog

Early on, my mom would call me (she still didn't know about email, thank God) and mention how Myspace was being discussed on Oprah. Why wasn't Facebook? Then, how Myspace and another site were talked about on the radio.

It's easy in retrospect to look back 10 years later and say of course this is how it would play out, but I don't think people give Mark enough credit. He single-handedly had to keep making good decisions, or at least, quickly fix bad ones over a 10-year period. I don't know anyone who has that patience.

A few major ones that come to mind:

→ He didn't give in to opening the site too early to allow everyone to join.
→ When Beacon was launched that shared some user information, Facebook quickly removed it and successfully re-launched the Facebook 'Like' button months later.

→ Monetizing the site. Mark was very patient about growing the business and focusing on that instead of rushing to make money (which I always advocated).

→ Mobile. In 2006, most sites weren't thinking of mobile traffic and Mark knew to start building that at least four years before mobile traffic with iPhones and Androids were significant to Internet businesses.

→ Platform. Mark recognized that he could have more developers to help grow the site and more engaged users via a platform. So, he spent years before launching the FB platform and very quickly updating it based on changes from the Facebook users.

→ Facebook newsfeed. This was light years before it seemed to make common sense to just have some smart stream of data showing what's going on with your surrounding friends.

Time erases most memories, but there were literally hundreds of social networks that made blunders of some sort from which they were never able to recover.

And even though we had raised over $10 million and had 5+ million users and were growing rapidly, nothing was guaranteed.

Do you recall that early on Google launched a social network and there was Yahoo! 360°? Ha, I know, but still they had 500+ million users combined and the ability to wipe this little college/high school social network out rather quickly — had they made the right decisions, but they didn't.

When we were only on the third floor and taking over the second floor in our Palo Alto office, there was a Chinese guy who had the other half of the floor. He ran an investment trading company.

When we were taking over the floor he asked me, "What is it that your company does?"

I described how we were a social network that helps connect people online, to imagine it like an online white pages which I found the easiest way to describe to people. It's funny to me that almost everyone knows what Facebook is now. Now you use Facebook to describe other things.

He chuckled and wondered how the hell we were going to make money and stay in business. Three months later, he was moving out of the space that we subsequently took over.

Promoting the Noah Brand

During that time, I definitely took advantage of the fact that a small group of people knew who the site was: early tech adopters who heard about it through their little brothers and their friends.

I spent time inviting outsiders into our office, like the two founders of box.net who were very goofy guys that I hung out with.

I'd also host the group I created at Intel to meet other entrepreneurs at the Facebook office.

I spoke at small techy conferences around Silicon Valley as a rep for Facebook.

On Okdork.com, my personal site, I would write articles about whatever new feature we just launched. We weren't discussing or letting the public know what we were doing and I took it upon myself to let the world know. I was excited to share what we were working on; it was the most important thing in the world in my eyes.

At the time, I did want the attention I received for being at Facebook. I wanted people to think of me as smart, I wanted to use the brand of a small but rapidly growing company to help me validate who I was as a person. I also wanted to talk about what I loved the most. Facebook.

Months 3 – 6

At Berkeley and Intel I never met the caliber of people I experienced when I was at Facebook. The level of attention to detail surprised me and influenced me while I was at the company.

Mark sent out emails saying how we were supposed to capitalize the F in Facebook. God forbid you'd spell it facebook, but learned to appreciate the consistency of that type of detail.

The designers would discuss at length which font type to use on a page. Who cares I would think? Aren't there more important things in the world like curing cancer or starvation? But these guys made it seem like it was the most important decision in the world and would talk about it all day.

Their influence has definitely stuck with me. I now notice when a site's copyright says 2013 instead of 2014. Mark or someone would have caught that. Precision mattered.

As we expanded the site, the #1 directive was growth. The features that helped us grow, we'd rush to build. Imagine creating your own restaurant, that's how we felt. A bit of that dish, move that chair over here, etc. The customer feedback was mostly ignored and the features we wanted we'd build as fast as possible, and fix it afterwards.

This was unlike the old-school Microsoft approach of hiring product managers to write out every product detail, debate them in a lot of meetings, and then finally build it, a painfully slow process. Then once you finally built the features, it'd taken too long or you learned you didn't even want them in that certain way.

A great way to see what a company values is by looking at the percentage of employees assigned to different departments.

At that time, Facebook had 50 people and here's how it looked:

→ 40% engineers
→ 20% system administrators
→ 20% customer service
→ 15% general administrative (accounting, marketing, HR)
→ 5% product managers

The company looked at engineers as gods and I still see it that way today. Engineers create. Everyone else's role is to support them as much as possible and remove anything in their way.

Here's how it felt to be working on the website at Facebook in 2005:

1. Mark tells you personally or tells your team what he wants.

2. We product managers write up details on how it should work and get approval from Mark. Often Mark would circumvent product managers and go directly to the engineers for a feature.

3. After we propose to Mark how we think the feature should work, he says it's shit, which after he showed why, he was almost always right.

4. You make the changes you think will satisfy his vision. Mark says it's shit again. You make more changes until Mark is happy, and then you go to the next step.

5. We collaborate with engineers, who did most of the work. Facebook did an amazing job hiring self-starters. Some needed handholding, but mostly, the team was amazing and could run without a product manager once the goal and parameters were made clear.

6. After you test the feature for bugs with the other product manager, you bring in the customer support team for testing and creating help material.

7. Get another approval from Mark before it goes live.

8. Feature goes live the same day he approves. You have to realize that most traditional companies were pushing new features once a month if that. Facebook was doing it multiple times a day. That pace was unheard of and we lived for it.

9. Monitor site feedback, look for bugs, and identify what's next for version 2.

Decisions were either top down, mostly from Mark, or bottom-up — led by a developer's proposal that resonated with Mark. No upper committee trying to figure things out and dictate to the people in the trenches. We'd bring ideas to Mark or just build them and show them to him, or we worked off a clear, "this needs to be done" order by him.

In the early days, engineers could still ship features that they thought were cool — and that weren't planned — without Mark's approval. Some of these unplanned products were Wall-to-Wall (posting on people's profile page walls) and adding a personal message with a friend request.

All I can say is that Mark could get pissed off when he found out that these features went live if he didn't like them. It was strictly his site and it was very clear to all that it was going to be his way. Sometimes he'd be okay with them; it wasn't always clear which way he'd go when he saw new features on the site.

The liberty we had to just push features enabled us to have more freedom and a feeling of ownership of the product. As an employee, a feeling of purpose is huge and being able to launch something and instantly see people using it is greatly satisfying.

So Who Was Mark Zuckerberg?

Lots of people ask me about Mark, what he's really like. I'll try to give you an idea.

Mark's eye for product perfection was relentless. I built some features as we transitioned Flyers into the Ads platform. It was a feature that helped people to figure out how much to spend on their budgets. There was easily two weeks invested in it. Despite that, Mark cut it the day before it was scheduled to go live. He had no problem cutting any feature he didn't think was right or good enough. This sucked. Sometimes he justified it and other times it was just his opinion. Yea, it pissed me off and made me feel insignificant, especially after spending a long time working on something.

I remember another product-related Mark story — this one a bit more action-oriented. While I don't remember the feature we were working on, engineer Chris Putnam and I had spent almost a month building something we thought Mark would love. He walks to Chris' computer and we demo the product for him.

Mark thought it was shit. I know so because instead of giving product feedback, he screamed, "This is shit — redo it!" threw water on Chris' computer and walked away. All of us stood around in shock. He normally didn't go off that hard. Needless to say, it definitely left an impression on all of us.

We made sure the next demo went more smoothly. We addressed his issues that he mentioned briefly. Sometimes he was a bit ambiguous with the directions. As much as this seems hard, it was always a culture of pushing yourself to be better. He may have been young and prone to temper tantrums, but he wanted the site to be the best and the biggest. That was his way for not apologizing and behaving in these ways.

Other times, he'd walk around with a samurai sword fake threatening to attack you for bad work. Where the hell he got that samurai sword, who the hell knows? Luckily, no employees were harmed while I was there. He'd come around and pretend to cut you, joking that if you took down the site he'd chop your head off. You have to remember, you have a 23-year-old uber nerd running one of the fastest growing sites on the web. As mature as he could be he was also still immature.

Beyond Mark's sign-off, there was another common thread weaved throughout the way things were done: an unbreakable set of "laws." I still vividly remember these six laws:

1. **Never say the word "user."** Ever. Mark would literally yell at you for using this word. It mattered to him and still sticks with me to this day. He wanted us to recognize the

users as people, not just a user, which he thought was belittling. In retrospect we did treat them more as users than human beings so I wasn't clear why this truly bothered him so much.

2. **Fix it...NOW!** Periods and commas are everything! Attention to detail, grammar and ease of use are the most critical things on the site. I even got an early Hanukkah present from Mark, the book *Elements of Style* by Strunk and White.[1]

3. **Trust yourself.** If you use the product, it makes it easier to know what works best. Almost all engineers and the majority of the employees were around the age of 24 and used Facebook, so it was easy to know what they wanted on the site.

4. **People don't know what they want.** Basically, never listen to the site visitors. The majority of people wanted the site to be so many random things. Such as fully customizable backgrounds, music playing when you load a profile page, being able to view the full information of everyone's profile (creeper!), and numerous other bad ideas.

Early on, we were receiving 10,000 pieces of feedback every day. It was impossible to read everything — and for the most part, we ignored everything. We read those comments out loud and laughed. The ideas were mostly ridiculous, so we let the users bitch and entertain us.

On a rare occasion, so many people would write in that Mark would consider making a change. Another way was if a friend of Mark's emailed him that something was wrong, he'd order us to change something back if he agreed. I realized that for the most part, only the complainers write in, and that people naturally resist change. Mark really did care about the users and chose to make features he believed would make their experience better. He just knew what he wanted for himself, so it was easy to provide it for others. When Facebook eventually launched Newsfeed, people were in an uproar about how it invaded their privacy and they liked the old Facebook.

Then a few weeks later, people were obsessed with the update to the site.

One of the interesting things about being on the inside was seeing how long something took to create versus when the public finally saw it. Newsfeed and the FB platform, for instance, were both two years in development before they went public. Some things took longer than others to develop.

5. **Don't suck.** There was some Google envy, though it wasn't envy exactly. This stemmed from Google being a very impressive company, having tons of revenue, and hiring really bright people. They launched their own social network, Orkut, which only had success in Brazil. That meant we were aiming to destroy and kill that social network.

We wanted to be the better and bigger company than them. It was more that we wanted to prove (not show) that we were better and more technical.

We tried to hire people that had offer letters from Google.

Facebook jokingly made our slogan "Don't suck." This was in direct contrast to Google's "Don't be evil," which we thought was just silly as we believed they could do evil things.

However, our official saying remained "Domination," which was toasted, shouted, and always preached in the company. What did it mean? It meant what it meant. As Mark defined it, we needed to achieve domination in the social networking space, that the world would be connected through Facebook, which is looking more and more the case.

6. **The site can never be down.** In the early days, Facebook prided itself on never crashing — something taken for granted nowadays. At the time, social networks had a reputation for frequently being down, because Friendster and Myspace had bad uptime problems. This was one of the reasons people speculated why Facebook was preferred.

To prevent any downtime, the Operations team was huge early on. Ten people worked around the clock, wearing Army gear for fun and were on call 24/7, which I'm sure their wives loved.

I learned over time that system administrators, aka "sys ops," are a very unique breed of guys. Most were introverted, loved Kevin Smith, *Star Wars*, driving exceptionally fast cars, and mostly learned computers through hacking in their high school years. They had girlfriends and wives who were as nerdy as them. Facebook had exceptionally bright people to deal with the billions of page views we were dealing with at the time. These guys had pagers, aka "wife #2," and someone would always have to be on call like a doctor if there was an issue with the site. They were some of the unsung heroes of Facebook as they only received attention if there were hiccups with the site.

We all tried to impress Mark with our work and dedication, attempting to be the alpha-nerds that he chose to keep in his inner circle.

A few people, like Aaron Sittig, Mark Slee, and a few others, could more or less do as they pleased within the company and with the website. That was a status we all desired.

Think of it like trying to get your dad's attention and doing whatever it takes for that. We did this by staying as late as possible, working on features unassigned to see if Mark would approve them, and surprisingly, challenging Mark. You'd think you'd go further in life agreeing with your boss, but the more you reasonably challenged his thoughts (with a good, logical argument) the more he liked you.

Complex Dynamics

As if navigating within this framework wasn't ambiguous enough, some complex dynamics emerged between the younger and older members of the office. Since Facebook had received nearly $40 million in venture capital money by that time, executives from Amazon, Yahoo! and Microsoft were brought in to provide adult supervision.

Mark, who was only 24 at this time, could still do whatever he wanted. The company resembled a combination of *Lord of the Flies* meets old-school Silicon Valley prestige.

In *Lord of the Flies*, these children have an island all to themselves. Same as Facebook, the "kids" got to run the show. We were on our own island with vast riches (from old investors) and had much older people taking orders from us. And every person wanted to impress Mark, who eternally owned the conch.

There were generally two internal camps of people: young and right out of college like me, and older people, like Jeff

Rothschild, the founder of Veritas (now sold to Symantec for $13 billion) and others, who provided the adult supervision. It may seem strange but we were running a business with over $40 million in funding. Can you imagine giving that to a 24 year old and trusting them? I couldn't at the time. Now it is more common and I believe with the appropriate guidance a 20-something can create and run a multi-billion dollar business.

These camps created some uncomfortable power dynamics. Mark, Dustin — even myself — and other younger team members would be telling older, vastly more experienced executives that they were wrong. It could be pretty uncomfortable, yet interesting, to watch the "children" around me (and including me) telling successful businessmen, such as Jeff Rothschild, that he was wrong or that there is another way to do things. Most of the adults took it in stride and loved Facebook as much as we did so they put up with us extremely, arrogant youngsters.

For example, you have someone like Owen Van Atta who was a VP at Amazon.com making a healthy salary with significant stock options now getting ordered around by a kid who dropped out of college. Sometimes, Owen would suggest things that Mark would just immediately shoot down. Over time, anything product-related would only be decided by Mark, while the "adults" had a bit more influence on every other aspect of the business (hiring, marketing, monetizing, etc.).

While older executives like Jeff had clout and people respected them, the final say always came down to Dustin or Mark. And, in general, their decision-making turned out to be correct. Adults were right in bringing on support staff to assist the company with marketing, accounting, hiring, and more, while Mark's decisions on the product were nearly always correct, and made the site grow more (which was also his directive).

This *Lord of the Flies* analogy also meant that people competed against each other. And we all looked down on all people outside of the company, as if they weren't lucky or good enough to be a part of this special experience. Each person in the company was vying for Mark's attention and to be the creator of the most influential parts of the website.

My former Facebook colleague, Karel Baloun, who was an "elder" and early engineer, said that this island lacked a conch. In other words, if you were physically present, you were worthy of being pulled into a meeting. If you weren't around, you practically didn't exist. It was that simple.

The Hidden Side of Building Facebook

As I look back, I think the dynamics between the "old" and "new" guard helped attract a mix of people that were hard-working, creative, gritty, brilliant, decisive, and fearless.

These people came together and created a series of cultural staples that persist to this day: hackathons, Easter eggs, and finding ways to make money in clever, unconventional ways.

My FAVORITE feature of working at the site was the ability to see who viewed your profile. I used to play this game where I'd poke my ex-gf, Nicole, and then see if she would see my profile. She always did and it made me feel free great. Don't worry, this feature was only available to employees. Sadly, due to privacy reasons this access was removed months later (or is it???).

The hackathon was an all-night coding adventure where you could drink as much Red Bull as possible and code something not within your normal day-to-day responsibilities. Basically, the developers could do whatever they wanted not related to their everyday work and complete it in only one night.

This was appealing for developers but as a non-technical person I felt obligated to be around to show face and wanted to contribute regardless. During the two hackathons I was a part of, I learned to code to be able to make things for the site that I've always wanted. This frustration, and the way I developed my subsequent skill, have helped me with many future projects, even to this day.

For our advertising platform, I personally created some internal graphs which helped show how much revenue we were making and progress bars when advertising to encourage people to spend more. I sometimes felt like the only one at the company who was focused on making sure we eventually had a solid business model. Maybe it was a residual effect of my Jewish father who didn't speak English, sold carpets to make a living, and eventually started a copier business that became moderately successful. My father had to pay for us and he made it clear he had to go work his ass off to provide that. It was instilled in me to be practical with money and from him that actual money pays bills.

One developer wanted to be able to add a message when you friend someone and that subsequently made it to the entire site after a hackathon.

The friend's game was also created, where you saw people's pictures and had to guess who said they liked a specific book or other things in their profile. This went live on the site for a short period of time.

The NCAA tournament fantasy brackets were conceived and designed during the hackathon. I even built an auto-poke feature where once I logged in, it auto-poked anyone who poked me so I didn't have to bother poking back. SO convenient but unfortunately never made it to the live site.

It was a really long and tiring night, but extremely fun. Most hackathons ended with a celebratory breakfast at IHOP. What more would you expect from a bunch of 24-year-olds?

At Facebook we loved to add hidden features that only internal people would know about. They're called Easter eggs. Why'd we do them? 'Cause it was fun and nerdly (that's a real word!) mischievous. There are tons on Google and other sites. Excel used to have a flight simulator. Naturally, Facebook couldn't be left out of copying what old-timers have done, and likely was an unconscious knock on Google always changing their doodle.

This was a great demonstration of how Facebook's culture led people to really want to own their piece of the site. Here's a few I recall (most still aren't active but they make me smile mentioning them):

Birthday Calendar: If you clicked on the center of the birthday box on the homepage, it would take you to a page with all of your friends' birthdays. This was really convenient to see all the upcoming ones. Nice work done by Jon at our all-night hackathon.

Petroleum: If you clicked on the word petroleum on the mobile.php page, it would show you a quail quote. The quail was a symbol we had on shirts and referenced often. It was from the movie, *Wedding Crashers*, and this was our own personal homage to it.

Quail: If you sent an SMS that read "quail" to Facebook mobile FBOOK 32665, you would get a movie quote of the day.

Fire: Initially thought to be an Easter egg, this gradually became a part of the product. Fire was a mobile poke. You would send a text message to Facebook mobile called "Fire (friend's name)," and this showed their status message on their profile on fire. The person could then log in and "extinguish" the fire.

Search: If you could find someone while searching with at least nine different criteria (hometown, age, gender, status, etc.), you'd get a special message on the bottom of the page.

You could see all of the pictures of your friends by going to your Friends tab and trying different things with the "Show:" dropdown.

Early, Unconventional Money-Making Strategies

We weren't super metrics driven at that time, but had an internal dashboard that showed how many new people signed up that day and how many total at that college were on the site. This was before the days of lean startup, big data, and AB testing being the default at companies. Mark and, subsequently, the company just wanted more signups. That was the only priority that mattered. It wasn't that we neglected them, but those types of metrics and optimizations that are so popular now weren't talked about at the time.

I was shocked at getting 50,000 signups a day and surprised Penn State was the largest college system we had at the time. Who knew that one college campus was so large? Seemed mind blowing to have so many people at one place.

Other data tools we looked at were how the site web servers were doing. The traffic we were receiving put us as one of the top sites on the web. The stats we were seeing internally were crazy: 75% weekly and 90% monthly login rates from eight million people. At the time, that level of engagement was unheard of.

Early on, Facebook was notoriously conservative about plastering the site with ads like Myspace. Mark wasn't focused on making money and thought that distracted from growing the site. Overall, Mark valued design over money and more ads would mean a less clean Facebook. Surprisingly, Facebook was profitable nearly from the start until we started hiring a ton of people.

Here are the three major strategies that brought in money:

Self-Service Advertising. The initial product was called announcements, and it allowed students to buy an advertisement that was shown to a certain percentage of students who logged into the site. It solved a HUGE problem on campus, where it's hard to capture students' attention and flyering billboards takes too much time.

I helped create the advertising version called Flyers and, subsequently, Facebook Ads. The pricing was a $5 minimum to students on their campus and $50 for businesses advertising to a campus. Students could choose templates to make their ad more attractive and use photos on the flyer to make it more appealing.

Sponsored Groups. Any large company could sponsor a group on Facebook. They'd get to have a large membership base, great advertising, and a chance to speak directly with their customers. Companies could customize their page, send out a few emails a month, and have students nationally talk about topics on a message board.

Advertising Networks. Companies such as advertising.com and doubleclick.net had tons of advertisers whose ads were placed on any of their partner sites. Facebook was a destination that had a lot of inventory (10 billion monthly views) and could handle serving tons of ads to students. I think Facebook sold these directly as well.

One-offs. Remember that NCAA tournament we created during a hackathon? The sales team was able to get some large companies to sponsor them.

For an advertiser, Facebook was a dream in targeting the college market. Think about how detailed you can target your advertising. You could promote a new movie to a gay Mexican in Texas that loved cooking and reading. Google was very good at helping people go somewhere else, but Facebook could pinpoint the exact people an advertiser would look for. It was a very good opportunity that more companies started to become aware of. That's why we all believed that with world domination would come world riches.

Mark was very sensitive to monetizing the site. One time I approached him with the idea to enable people to sell tickets through our event pages. He taught me something I have never forgotten. On a white board, he wrote the word "growth" and nothing else. He said if any feature didn't help do that then he was not interested and the idea was crushed. That was the only priority that mattered and his singular focus on accomplishing something has stuck with me till today. We had to do maintenance to the site, but all the big changes and things we worked towards were catching up and surpassing Myspace and taking over the world for connecting people. Singular focus — it helped us all stay on track, all the time.

It was interesting to observe Mark and Dustin's relationship with money during our time together. They took "cash off the table," which is when founders of successful startups sell some of their shares for equity to investors so they have less risk for going big. They wouldn't have to worry about the company selling since they would then have a few million dollars in the bank.

Mark and Dustin did this and it didn't seem to change them much. Dustin had a 6 Series BMW and surprisingly sold that quickly to purchase a Toyota 4Runner, while Mark drove a humble Infiniti FX45 SUV. Both of these non-showy cars that young multi-millionaires bought left an impression on me. Neither of them was about the money; they loved Facebook and the money was a nice perk that came along from their important creation.

I recall one specific day. I was already at Facebook for months and got restless. I couldn't imagine spending my whole life or even five years working on the same thing. So I asked Dustin what he wanted to do in five years. I never forgot the answer.

"Facebook."

My Contributions to Facebook

As a product manager, my responsibility was to make sure the "product happened." That included finalizing features, discussing (aka arguing) with Mark, informing everyone in the company about new features being built, organizing the features, helping the people working on new products, looking for any bugs in the code, fixing issues after reviews with Mark, and monitoring feedback and bug reports when it was launched.

When you're working at a startup, you have to be ready to work on everything. There's no "I can't learn to do that." It's more like, "Shit, how will I learn how to code this page in a day?" There were times when I could've asked an engineer to do something, but that would have taken him away from doing something important. So, I read some books, checked things out online, and coded a lot of the help section. This self-starter spirit was idealized at Facebook, and only people who kept taking initiative stayed around to help the business grow.

Status

Way back in the day, Facebook used to let you connect your AOL Instant Messenger account to show your status. Remember that?

I knew you didn't.

Hardly anybody used it, so we removed the feature. This was an amazing skill of Mark's — he let go of his ego. We'd spend weeks on a feature like this and then, if he felt it wasn't helpful, he'd just ask for it to be removed. No emotional attachment.

But after we killed it, I couldn't shake this nagging feeling that Facebook was too static. It seemed to ask people "What have you been doing?" but not "What *are* you doing?"

I went to Dustin Moskovitz and proposed that we let people say what they were doing in real-time. Part of my pitch was that it gave people a reason to come back to the site more often and share what's going on with them and their friends.

Keep in mind this was before Twitter was ever invented. Twitter's earliest, most elementary form, actually came out three months after Status launched.

Dustin was skeptical since the AIM away message seemed similar to this and was eventually removed due to low usage; he didn't want to put this feature out there to a similar fate. Instead of debating theoretical scenarios, we agreed that if 10% of people used it post-launch that we would keep the feature. Many times in companies, egos get in the way where both people think they are right. To this day, I still use this method where I propose a small test with a specific result and let that make the decision.

At that time, we never released products to the entire site. We always released them to specific college campuses to make sure the server load was okay and that the feature didn't have too many bugs.

Being highly motivated to get Status out the door, I worked with a single developer and got the feature live within a week.

Status had a huge amount of usage. I was proud when it was subsequently rolled out to the rest of the Facebook network. It's now obviously one of the most prominent features on Facebook across desktops and mobiles. I never rubbed it in Dustin's face and appreciated him letting me build and test it versus just rejecting it immediately.

This is the power of "Facebook the organization." It's a combination of Mark's persistence and perfection, a culture that encourages creativity, experimenting with ideas, breaking things at fast speeds, and a small group of talented people creating a tool benefitting millions of people.

Mark Seeing the Future

Mark is a visionary. In 2006, he asked me to organize a place where people could put anything. "What the hell does that mean?" I thought to myself. In retrospect, it's obvious — online pages that represented non-humans. This is what everyone knows now as Pages where brands, artists, and businesses can host a page on Facebook. This was two years before they even went live. It was his future vision of how to get businesses more involved within Facebook. It was to be pages where, instead of personal identities, celebrities, businesses, and more could display themselves and connect with their fans. It was the last thing I worked on.

This was a difficult task for me to organize. I had to figure out how we were going to categorize the types of pages, which sections per each page, and how it would compare to a user's profile. It seems obvious as you use it now, but there wasn't really anything extremely comparable. Myspace had some crappy pages for brands that mirrored a user's profile, but it wasn't very engaging. I never got to see my plans nor work on this going live.

Mobile was just as visionary. Mark essentially said "go do it." That's about all the direction we got. This is before responsive design and even the iPhone was out. Most people assumed mobile usage was in poor Third World countries, and Internet speeds were so slow that nobody realized the mobile web's full potential.

I partnered with Mark Slee, one of the best programmers with whom I'd ever worked, to build it. We tried to filter it down to the three features that most people would want to do while away from their computers: add friends, poking, and look up a friend's profile info.

We launched it within a week, and instantly, millions of people were using it. To celebrate, I remember company executives treated us to a $1,000 meal in Las Vegas on the company's dime.

Opening Facebook up to "Outsiders"

(high school and corporate emails)

Most people forget that Facebook was started only for people with .edu for such a long time. Mark recognized the larger demographics and tasked us with doing that switch. It was much larger than people realize because there were attributes of profile, search, and more that were based on college students.

It took a 10-member team months for both groups to be able to allow high school students to join Facebook.

At first there was a ton of negative backlash from college students. Mark would not budge and it wasn't just a feature we could revert. Ultimately, it was the right call as it was the beginning of opening Facebook up to the rest of the world. It was confusing working there at times when Mark and our culture were rushed, and at the same time, very thorough so things like this process took months before we released it.

Mark ultimately spent a lot of time alone thinking through his decisions. It seemed strange to me at the time, but it definitely helped him think through strategy and imagine what Facebook could become.

Creating Facebook Search

In realizing that corporate networks were coming, we had to improve search. (Corporate networks were ONLY referred to as work networks since corporate was too...corporate.) A brilliant programmer named Aditya from CMU developed the whole thing. How many engineers at Google does it take to work on their search? Probably 500+ would be my guess.

Facebook, which handled millions of searches a day, had one guy. He spent about three months working non-stop on the product, fleshing out the features, developing the server structure, and thinking of everything.

Looking back over the journals I kept at the time, I now realize how frenetic the pace really was. We kept crazy build schedules — almost daily product updates — and rarely backed off of it. The pace certainly took its toll on my friendships, many of which withered and died during my time at Facebook. I hardly hung with any of my old Intel or Berkeley friends except at birthday parties.

But I loved every minute of it. We were growing at a daily rate of 50,000 new student signups. And we were on track for our world domination.

Mark's Quirks

With anything we launched, tens of thousands of comments and feedback poured in from our customers. Most of them were complaints or requesting some Myspace-like features, which we completely ignored. Mark consistently described Facebook as a way for people to connect, and less about being an expression of creativity. I internalized his statements, always thinking of Facebook as a modern-day white pages.

It was through this experience that I learned from Mark the importance of sticking to one's guns. He taught us to wait and see how comments stacked up over time: if they faded and usage remained the same, then no course correction was smart. But if the complaints continued over a long period of time, changes might be warranted. This taught me a valuable lesson that many times the users didn't know what they wanted until we showed it to them.

Mark was exceptionally gifted, well-reasoned, and patient despite the adrenaline and chaos around him. He wasn't just lucky — as many people to this day still believe — but he worked hard and devoted his life to Facebook. Because of his dedication and focus, he grew so much in such a short period of time, from being able to hire a team, prioritizing the features to build, and encouraging specific people to step-up and help lead Facebook and more. Witnessing this development firsthand was amazing.

Everyone around the office revered him. His speech was very slow and deliberate to the point you were waiting for what he'll say next, so we knew every word was important. Thoughts emerged from him that were on a different plane than almost anyone I'd ever known. And his great quirks were widely appreciated.

I still remember the day he first described to me what would become of the Facebook platform. He started describing a "black space" where people could do anything they wanted to Facebook.

I remember going, "Huh?"

Mark said, "Yeah, they'd have a space where anything could be created. Like some alternative Facebook for themselves." I truly thought he was nuts at that time, but in a few years, the platform would go on to create billion dollar businesses like Zynga.

He also gave frequent speeches about how we were doing. At the end of them, he usually led a cheer — it was always to (world) domination.

I vividly remember the speech where he told us that he rejected Yahoo's billion dollar offer. He made clear to everyone that this business was something special and not just about making money. We were all shocked at his intensity. He described how Facebook would become a large business. I suppose it seems more obvious now, but at the time it wasn't clear. "We'll have the world be the destination," he said, "and we'll be a tollbooth taking small pieces along the way." I wasn't disappointed since I knew we'd be even bigger and my stock would be worth way more money. It was nice in retrospect with a leader having a strong conviction and vision.

For his 24th birthday, all of us guys wore Mark's signature Adidas sandals. The few ladies we had at the office wore t-shirts of Mark's face. It was strange but we idolized our leader; not sure if this happened at all companies, but it was nice to pay homage to him.

He had some great motivational lines. With love, he'd say, "If you don't get that done sooner, I will punch you in the face," or "I will chop you with this huge sword," while holding a huge sword in hand.

Without question, his heart, life, and every moment were dedicated to Facebook — and creating a tool to help information flow and connect everyone. What's taken as cliché, PR-ridden drivel today actually started out true. Facebook's mission, driven by Mark, has been from the start "to connect the world."

Mark didn't always want to be in the spotlight. Regardless, he received more attention with the increasing success of

Facebook. He's an anti-social person by nature, which is strange given that he created a site that helps people connect with the people they know (and meet new people). What confused me was that unlike everyone in the company, he chose not to add the Facebook logo on the messenger bag everyone received for Christmas.

Mark himself was a minimalist, but made sure the office spared no expense for the people building his company. When I first arrived, there were decent chairs, hardcore desks, 24-inch flat panels for everyone, and a PowerBook with my name on it. And after receiving nearly $40 million in funding, the office underwent a multi-hundred-thousand-dollar redesign.

I remember when I first heard that we were getting a $500,000 office makeover, I thought this was a huge waste of money for a company not making any and voiced my concerns. But Mark was steadfast about what he wanted to do.

He recognized early on (which I completely missed) that having a work environment you want to work at would appeal to potential employees and make the existing ones that much more proud to be there (and stay later at night).

"I want the employees to have a great place to be in. That is also why we are located in the heart of downtown Palo Alto," Mark said.

He figured that paying $20,000+ month in rent was a pricey luxury, but allowed us to work in a great location. It was all about making people want to work there. Chairs that cost $1,000 each were considered a must for the whole office. I was used to working out of a dorm room (no startup pun intended) and being resourceful. Spending so much on furniture was foreign to me.

Compared to the office, his nearby Palo Alto apartment at the time seemed like poverty to me. It had a small bed, some clothes (mostly his signature Patagonia jacket, jeans, Adidas sandals, an assortment of Facebook t-shirts), and a teapot. That's it! No TV, barely any dishes or utensils, hardly any food, and I don't even think there was Internet.

The minimalism reflected his personal preference and why Facebook, the website, is as minimal as possible.

The one time I visited the apartment, we sat on the floor, drank green tea, and talked about Facebook. As usual, I always felt nervous about impressing him and this conversation was no different.

At the office, he had his own room that I called "The Matrix." It was an eerily all-white room with a white table, two whiteboards, and white chairs. He used this as his main meeting room and spent time diagramming things on the white board for people who met with him.

One thing at the time that confused me was how Mark had some old lady following him around. I asked who it was and someone said it was an executive coach. It seemed silly we should be listening to some old lady.

In retrospect, he had the foresight to hire this person and utilize her. It definitely helped him think through decisions in growing the company. It likely helped him learn how to hire better and have more empathy towards the people he was working with. What we were doing with 30 people he couldn't be doing with 150 and even now with 2,500+ employees.

Mark was always open to listening and making a final decision. His ability to add people and immediately remove people is one of his strongest skills. He removed people immediately who were holding Facebook back and quickly promoted the ones who were helping it achieve success.

Mark's Office Perks

I would've literally worked for free at Facebook because of the things I got to do there. However, I was paid better, and received more stock options and more ridiculous perks than at Intel.

Leaving Intel for Facebook was a huge transition. My mom was confused why I gave up the great benefits and prestige of a large company to work at a startup. My grandmother was completely lost on what I did all day.

Facebook's penchant for hyper-competitive salaries also extended to the environment and perks. Spending was never a concern there.

Any parking tickets were paid in full. For the first few months, most received one or two a day. Mark believed the convenience of not having to deal with parking meters outweighed the cost to the company. The city of Palo Alto was definitely a huge fan of ours.

Breakfast, lunch, and dinner were catered by one of the best, Gramercy Park Catering. Definitely made Google food look pathetic.

Any type of drink you can imagine, except Naked Juice, which was so delicious and only found for free at the Googleplex. Damn you, Google.

Every engineer and customer support person received a BlackBerry. At the time, these were $300 phones that had a monthly charge of $80 – $100. The company must've been burning $75,000+ a year just on mobile phones.

All-expense-paid trips to Las Vegas. When we launched Facebook Mobile in 2006, we celebrated with a $1,000 dinner. That was definitely worth it.

Free happy hours. Every Friday, we would be smothered with wine, beer, and Framboise (a delicious French sweet beer you should definitely try). We would have deviled eggs, stuffed mushrooms, beef, chicken, shrimp, bread, cheese, chips with salsa and guacamole, and other amazing assortments provided by our caterer.

Purple Tie. This was a concierge-style service that's available at many companies, and does your laundry, dry cleaning, and photo development, among other things. Most companies subsidized or let you pay full price, but Facebook took it to the next level. Everything was covered. We had to pay taxes on what we used, but Facebook paid for all their services. I knew a lot of people who snuck laundry and dry cleaning in from friends and family.

Summer housing. Towards the beginning of summer 2006, Facebook announced they'd be getting a house for up to six people to live. This place had an amazing pool, tons of rooms, and was close to the office. It also had a rope slide where you could swing down from one of the bedrooms and land in the pool.

Winter cabin. For six months, Facebook rented a cabin in Lake Tahoe that anyone could use with friends for vacationing. Most of the stories involved lots of alcohol, drugs, and weekend romps at Squaw or Heavenly ski resort.

Subsidized living. Anyone who lived within one mile of the office could get $600 a month towards their living expenses. A few of us were thinking of buying a place and putting the money towards our mortgage. Executives like Mark or Dustin didn't get the credit.

Again, Mark never saw this spending as something excessive. He wanted to use the company's resources to simplify people's lives and to take care of everything else. This had the effect of making distractions less important so we could focus on work.

It was about dedicating our lives to the company. This sounds creepy but it's all everyone who worked there wanted to do. Every new benefit meant that Mark was looking out for us so we could focus on the fun things in life, which frankly was working on Facebook and hanging out with co-workers.

In retrospect it would have been nice to have more balance with outside interests, but I truly believe as we go through life, the work-life balance changes depending if we are working on something interesting, our age, our other relationships, and more. At that time, the balance was all work and I loved it.

Facebook from 30 to 100 People (months 6+)

The company inevitably got bigger. We just had to hire more people. I was struggling as meetings changed from me walking over to Mark's desk to make a quick decision, to having to schedule a time via Mark's secretary who sat between us, to then having 30 people to discuss new upcoming features. I was getting restless, and the larger and slower processes started to grind on me. Why am I listening to this old marketing bitch discuss things when she hardly gets Facebook?

And projects got more complex than I could handle or was interested in. I was starting to have to deal with massive Excel spreadsheets, just like at Intel.

One specific incident I recall was refactoring the code. It sounds boring because it mostly is.

Let me back up and explain: The whole idea comes from the fact that we moved quickly, so not all the code was as efficient as it could be. Think of it like creating a house out of wood and the fire season starts in 12 months. The wood is a good way to validate that people want to live there, but the house won't sustain into the future. So, refactoring the code means going back through how you originally built something and making it more efficient and effective. At the size and pace Facebook was growing with over 50,000+ new signups a day, and over 50% of our users coming back daily (not sure if you realize, but that's almost unheard of anywhere on the web, even today), managing was a bitch.

Ezra owned that project and got a massive Excel spreadsheet. Many developers organized to help refactor the entire site.

I knew I couldn't do it and was glad he had that project. I was still stuck in pandemonium and small-scale mode, while these guys were getting ready for world domination (yes, I know we used this word too much, but hey, Facebook succeeded).

The Harsh Reality of Working at Facebook

Sometimes by focusing so much on the work, we lost sight of everything outside of growing Facebook. Everything else in our lives was insignificant compared to that. One unfortunate moment for me at Facebook was the death of Dan Plummer. It was one part of the culture that negatively stayed with me to this day in a starkly negative way.

Dan Plummer was a quiet guy who kept to himself. He enjoyed studying graph theory, working through hardcore mathematical equations, and riding his bike. Dan was an ultra techie. He worked on analyzing all that sexy, sexy data that we treasured so greatly. He loved data, and Facebook sure had enough of it since people filled out tons of interesting information about themselves, which we could study to produce great things.

One day while riding his bike in the woods of Los Altos, a branch fell and killed him. Dan was a serious biker who spent most of his free time riding. What a freak accident. How could this have happened?

"Hey, did you hear Dan died bike riding?" someone said.

"Huh, shit," was the most common reaction in the office.

I think for all the young people in the office this was a huge surprise. Dan was well liked but flew under most people's radar.

To commemorate his passing, I was expecting a day off work where we'd go for a bike ride together, add a bike rack outside our office, something, anything.

Instead, there was a ceremony from one of his friends for just 15 minutes. Immediately afterwards, everyone went back to work like a normal workday. It was almost as if he never existed or contributed at the company. That bothered me, and I thought we could have spent a little more time commemorating Dan's life.

It made me realize if I were to die, there would be a very short-lived mourning period at Facebook. What is left of Dan is an empty profile and a quote he left on December 11th, 2005 at 9:34 pm:

"Warm days and cool nights training in the Santa Cruz mountains. Not much rain...yet." Facebook was bigger than any one person; even if Mark passed we'd keep going. Unfortunately, I realized the culture we created was that nothing would get in the way of Facebook, including myself.

SO Why Did I Actually Get Fired from Facebook

I was fired from Facebook. I have never shared the actual reasons why I got fired. Maybe I never clearly grasped why I was fired. Maybe I was ashamed of myself. Maybe I didn't want to recognize the mistakes I made and the embarrassment I felt from my actions. So why share now? Therapy. Sharing my story about my rise, fall, and subsequent "re-rise" hopefully can help you find the inspiration to keep going, even if bad things happen or you feel doubt about yourself. I know this book has helped me.

To the best of my knowledge I believe I was fired for four reasons:

I leaked knowledge to TechCrunch. I was at Coachella with a group of Facebook employees. It was night and I was alone by myself. Mogwai was performing some amazing music and I was intoxicated. We were launching the professional network (allowing people with corporate emails to join the site) at 9:00 am the next morning. The marketing people (who I had no respect for) had no plan to get the word out to corporate people about joining our site. I do think that's part of the arrogance we had at Facebook. We thought everything would work.

Instead of hoping, I decided to let TechCrunch know. At this time, it was a small feature that was launching in the morning. I talked to Michael Arrington and asked him to write about our launch in the morning.

Thirty minutes later, I was checking my BlackBerry and saw he published the article that night instead of in the morning as we agreed. FUCK. Instantly, I knew my ass was going to get chewed out for that.

At that moment, I emailed the entire executive team and let them know what happened. I am proud I took responsibility for what happened but didn't think it would ultimately lead to me getting fired.

Michael Arrington mildly apologized but I can't really blame him for what he did or what I shared.

I didn't really hear much from the e-team until a few weeks later when I was ultimately fired.

Do I regret making that call? Yes. But it happened. I can't go back in time.

I believe we justify the outcomes in our life to help rationalize that all our decisions were meant to be. I got to work with so many more people, work all over the world, and do so much more than I would have if I stayed at Facebook.

Would I take back my time at Facebook? Never. I grew so much with my technical skills, and learned how hiring great people can make an insanely large difference and driving towards a meaningful goal can help motivate a large group of people.

Self-promotion. While at Facebook I was writing blog posts on okdork.com, bringing in my friends to meet Mark and check out our offices, and hosting conferences for entrepreneurs. Why?

Because I loved our company and was so proud to show it off to other people.

One day, a few months after being at the company, Mark sat me down outside of the elevator and asked me to choose between myself and Facebook.

I loved Facebook more than anything but also loved promoting my own brand at the same time. Ultimately, everyone at the company chose to promote the company and recognized that Mark was the only person who was going to get the press.

This incident scarred me, up until a year ago when I was very apprehensive about putting myself out in the public light with business. Mentally, I associated putting myself first and in the public light with getting fired from being at Facebook.

After Facebook, I made it very clear to myself that I had to put the company first. I still think that is the best way to build your brand. Build great things and then people will be curious about the person made those products.

Professional network snafu. I was working with Dustin Moskovitz on deciding which companies were going to be able to join our professional network. We needed to choose the company domain names (@microsoft.com, @intel.com, etc.) that were going to be able to join Facebook.

I floundered on this project.

In trying to figure out which companies I should contact, I searched Google for a list of companies. After a week of pulling together names, it was a smorgasbord of random companies with no rhyme or reason to their order.

I presented this list to Dustin. He, of course, was disappointed to have waited and then been presented with a list of companies that wasn't comprehensive or well-organized.

At that point, he ran some database queries and aggregated companies based on the company domains we already had registered on the site, adding people to the waitlist who couldn't join yet.

Yes, that was much smarter.

Yes, I was disappointed I didn't think of that first.

Yes, I try to think about how to use frameworks or better ways to organize things versus my scattered ass way I did 10 years ago.

Evolving with the company.

When it was chaotic and things needed to get done, I was one of the best people in the company. I struggled with projects that dealt with multiple people, organizing a few months' build schedule and dealing with politics.

This experience has forever altered the way I handle firing people — it's changed how I would otherwise treat someone when I let them go from my own businesses.

Leading up to this moment, I would be remiss if I didn't point out that the months prior I wasn't really loving Facebook. Things had become more bureaucratic, yes.

The company was maturing — and I was still stuck in the college years.

Writing the conclusion to this story pains me. It's one of those experiences in life that I don't have photos of, but I can recall it in vivid detail.

During that last meeting, Matt Cohler called me a "liability." That phrase and the idea that I had the potential to fuck things up haunted me for years. I became insanely defensive whenever I had the potential to be a liability or possibly fuck things up in my personal life or other companies I was a part of. This was also a blessing because I became more conscious when working on things, constantly asking myself if I'm adding value to the situation. Thanks Matt!

Therapy Post-Facebook

After Facebook, I was really depressed. One of the worst things about it was thinking of all the money I would never see.

In Silicon Valley, one has to typically stay a year to get one-fourth of your options (a "cliff"), then the rest "vests" in quarter chunks for each year thereafter. Given that I stayed for a year, I could have fought to get those options. But Owen van Natta, Facebook's COO, said no and shut me down at the local Starbucks. In my mind, I justified that I didn't earn or deserve the equity that hadn't yet vested. Why didn't I fight harder?

I was embarrassed, I was uncertain of what to do. I wanted to put my head in the sand and wake up when the nightmare was over.

In retrospect, I could have made a stink like another person at the company who did upon getting fired and walked away with 100,000 shares ($6,000,000+ today). I wasn't so lucky.

With how much time I dedicated to Facebook, it felt like I worked there 10 years. One of the most helpful things to get through this period was a suggestion by Zynga founder, Mark Pincus. He suggested meeting a business coach "therapist."

During these sessions, I described how bitter I was about not having all the money my peers were soon to get. My coach suggested that I write down all the things I wanted to buy with the Facebook money I would have gotten when the company went public.

So, I went home and wrote the following:

1. BMW M3
2. A house
3. ?

I brought back the list and we went over it.

The exercise made me realize that I actually had everything I wanted to buy — that money wasn't really going to make my life better. It was this exercise and subsequent realization alone that helped me let go of the anger every time someone got bummed that I never got my equity.

The deeper issue was my new lack of identity as my life was Facebook. My "friends," or so I thought, worked there, while all of my non-FB colleagues knew where I worked and the pride I personally had in this company had been taken away.

It was a huge disappointment to have something stripped

from you, something that you associated with your self-worth. A good reminder to do "ego diversification," where you diversify the things that define you (gym, religion, reading, etc...) and focus on the ones that you can control.

There are two ways I was able to handle this situation after recognizing it wasn't just the money.

1. Look for something else to distract myself.

In a bit, you can read all the things I did to do that. Ultimately, I really tried to spend time on things and people that genuinely interested me — healthy distractions. I also attempted to minimize the amount of drinking and "mind distractions," which would have made reality easy to avoid.

2. Not do anything and take time to see what I could learn from what went wrong.

This is the harder one. I sat around, I jogged, I wrote, I did coffee with real friends. I wanted to learn why I was a "liability" and what I wanted for the future.

I didn't want something stripped from me without my control. I wanted discipline so that I produced things with great quality.

I wanted to work with people who truly cared about me, and if I wasn't around, they'd ask what happened.

I wanted to be at a company where I significantly mattered and focused on building the company, not just my own brand.

After Facebook

As if it wasn't immediately obvious, ending my relationship with Facebook was like the love of my life kicking me to the curb. I was stunned and didn't know what to do next.

The first thing I did was to cancel my Facebook account.

My next phase was what I called being "sad-employed."

During this time, I went to Korea to teach business on Jeju Island for two weeks. It was a pretty fun experience as I taught business, some English, and improved my karaoke skills.

I also did some consulting with Chris Dury of Scanr. He hired me since I had Facebook on my résumé. I'm grateful to him for helping me regain confidence in my product talent. We're friends to this day.

I also coordinated a number of conferences about social networks called CommunityNext.com.[2]

I had never coordinated events before and was interested in social networks so I invited the top sites of those days: Plenty of Fish, Hot or Not (James Hong), PayPal/Slide (Max Levchin), Suicide Girls, Threadless founders, and more. This conference took two months of work and I have close friends to this day that I met through this experience. It was a ton of fun and one of things I'm most proud of accomplishing in my life.

One thing that's stuck with me is to solve your own problems in starting a business. You understand the problems the customer (yourself) faces and the ideal solution versus having to do market research. Also, it is much easier to persist with that business when times are tough. Compare that to a fad or an opportunity where, as times get tough, you don't generally care for the outcome of that business besides the money it provides.

Six months later, Dave McClure asked me to come check out MyMint.com (now known as Mint). It was a personal finance tool I had heard about, but didn't know any details.

Aaron Patzer, Mint's founder and CEO, spent six months in his room coding it by himself. I met him once briefly at a Women 2.0 event and he came off as arrogant and rude. It rubbed me the wrong way and I almost didn't go to this meeting, but I love personal finance so I went.

I saw the product and instantly fell in love. On top of that, there was a huge market. Everyone wants to save or make more money. Even better, the whole product was free. I wanted to get involved.

The only open position was Director of Marketing. I knew I was under-qualified. I'd never done the job officially before in my life. I even referred other friends who didn't get the job.

So, I took a risk and told Aaron that I wanted it for myself. He flat out told me "No." I took another approach — I'd create a 90-day marketing plan. There'd be no cost and no risk to him. If he liked it, he could hire me as a contractor to execute it. And if I executed it well, I'd come on as a full-time employee with equity.

I'm happy to say it worked out well. I got hired as #4 at Mint. com as Director of Marketing and the company went on to sell to Intuit for $170 million. Additionally, I grew to appreciate and respect Aaron for his confidence.

But...I quit before the sell and didn't get my equity again.[3] "What a dunce," you're thinking. "How could he have made the same mistake twice?" So few people get the chance to be on one rocket ship and I was fortunate enough to be on two very hot companies very early on. Again, many of my colleagues went on to be multi-millionaires and I just went.

So why did I do it? Because of simple math and doing what I really wanted, my own business.

1. At Mint, I was given 1% of the company. At the time we were valued at $20 million, so my shares were "worth" $200,000. I expected the company to sell for around $200 – $500 million. Let's take the best-case scenario of $500 million.

1% of that is $5,000,000 but don't get too excited.

The company did take another round of financing at $100 million before that ever happened, which means that I would own less of the company. So take the total now to .5%, which is about $2,500,000. State taxes in California are 10% + 30% federal taxes, meaning I'm left with $1.5 million. Now that may sound like a lot but I'd have to "vest" (remember that evil word from my Facebook days) and stick with the company for another 3.3 years.

So, at that point, I assumed I could make at least a million in the next three years doing something for myself.

2. My ultimate goal has always been to work for myself, just like my dad. At Mint I was never going to be able to do that. In addition, I wasn't learning anymore. I had the chance to take a product without any traction or visibility and create more website traffic than all of our competitors before we even launched. There was nothing more for me to grow or learn regardless of the six-figure salary I was getting.

With those two key things in mind, I made the judgment call to leave after 9 months.

Was it tough? Not really.

At night, after a year of banning Facebook from my life, I noticed the Facebook platform open up and outside developers could add widgets to the site. Then, my friend, Amit Gupta, built an app that enabled people to showcase their favorite books on their profile. The neat thing he did, which was the light bulb going off, was that he had Amazon affiliate links attached to each of the books. At that time, I knew most Facebook profiles got around 50 page views a day. That number multiplied by the number of people who'd install it seemed like it could generate a nice chunk of cash each month.

After getting fired from Facebook, I was more determined to be smarter in my decision-making. Instead of just making any app, I tried to use a framework like Dustin did in choosing the domains for the Professional Network.

My criteria were:

A Had to be able to link to a relevant product on Amazon so I could attach affiliate links;
B Had to have international appeal; and
C Had to be in a category with the least amount of competing apps.

After reviewing all the categories I saw that 'sports' was the best opportunity. Then I noticed that the #1 app was called "Soccer Fan" and you could put your favorite team logos on your profile.

#lightbulb

What about the other sports? And what if you could also link to the sports team merchandise on Amazon?

A friend referred an outsourcer from the Philippines and I

had him duplicate the Soccer Fan app, but instead, we did it for Hockey.

I proceeded to create Facebook apps with a $20/hour outsourcer in the Philippines.

Then another outsourcer in India grabbed all the Hockey team logos from Wikipedia.

We put those together over my vacation weekend in Denver and it was launched on a Friday. Within seven days that single app had over a million installations.

I was on to something.

This is something I've learned for myself, and is valuable advice for all other burgeoning entrepreneurs.

Don't quit your day job. If you hate your job, that should motivate you to stay up later or get up earlier. Work weekends if you are really serious. There's no point jeopardizing your livelihood until you are nearly certain that what you are working on is, indeed, working.

So, once this app worked, I made it for all the other sports teams and then made it for the top 10 TV shows at the time.

This started generating around $3,000/month for me.

It was crazy. I remember during lunch breaks I would have to sneak upstairs to yell at my server guys since the amount of traffic I was doing couldn't be handled on the tiny computers I was sharing.

This side business was working and created the final comfort for me to take the leap from Mint and finally go full-time on my own business.

One thought that's stuck with me is how you, the reader, relate or not to this guy who seems to have bad luck in sticking with companies. Or, as my friend Jonathan Abrams said, every company should hire me, fire me, and then they'll make it big. The point is that all of us, including you, have gone and are going through tough times.

I'm not trying to say that mine are worse or better than yours. I'm hoping that by sharing this story that you will see that you should always be doing what you want, and that by moving forward with perseverance, even when it seems most dark, will take you to a better place. This is your life and it's up to you how you want it to be played out.

One of the ultimate things I realized as I was eating barbecue in Austin, Texas today (May 2, 2014) was how you move forward with what seems like life-ending situations, when it's impossible to see the light at the end of the tunnel. Maybe by reading this story, people will be able to realize there will be brighter days.

As much as I still feel pain, I do rationalize today that the Facebook ending opened me up for such a wide world of experiences I would have never had. Speaking at a business conference in Russia, working at AppSumo.com with some of my now closest friends, and being able to work from Argentina are among many other experiences.

It's not to say that I wouldn't have continued to have a great time at Facebook, but I have noticed that a few of the people who aren't working there anymore ("retired") seem lost. What do you do when you get that money you've always wanted?

When a "bad" thing occurs, the key point is to process the pain, LEARN for the next experience, and know it will get better. It always does. Remember after you broke up with your first significant other and you never thought you'd meet someone better. You always do.

Ultimately, keep asking yourself what you truly want. Every other week during therapy (highly recommended), I pay a guy $180 to have him repeat back to me what I really want. If young Noah were to guess what old Noah would be doing, he'd kick him right up the ass. Why do you need a shrink? It's less about the shrink and more about the chance to know myself better. Learn what truly motivates me, learn what I really want to be doing each day, explore why I wrote this book, and understand what the real root problem was that I felt post-Facebook.

For me, it's living in Austin, Texas, working on AppSumo, writing about marketing on Okdork.com, and doing my Friday bike rides to eat Tacos with my good buddy, Anton.

Notes

1. http://okdork.com/wp-content/uploads/2012/09/Mark-Zuckerberg-Note.jpg
2. http://okdork.com/2010/09/01/how-we-made-over-100k-doing-tech-events
3. http://okdork.com/2013/06/25/why-i-quit-mint-com-and-lost-out-on-1-7-million

Epilogue

It's funny how I heard that my manager who fired me was let go just three months afterwards. That was the chaotic life at Facebook.

My heart used to race thinking of Facebook and anger would just fill my veins. Revenge was all I could think of. That drove me to work harder and validate myself as a "successful" person.

I avoided writing this book for seven years.

After I published the article about why I got fired on Okdork, Erin Burnett from CNN asked to interview me. Huh? That was years ago. Why would anyone care?

I guess people like knowing that others have it worse than them. You sickos!

I was nervous as hell, but the interview went fine. The interview went so fast and made me reflect on how long ago that entire experience actually was. Almost seemed so old that it was another life. Time definitely heals wounds.

As my friend Tucker said about writing this book, it has been therapeutic and less painful than I imagined.

Amazing how what we avoid for so long and finally face doesn't seem as challenging as we created it in our minds.

I avoided sharing my story for so long since I wanted attention for doing great things, not for failing as I looked at my time at Facebook.

Now, with this book, I get to share that even with good and bad times things will get better. Persevere.

The time after Facebook was easily one of the lowest points in my entire life. It's as if the love of my life said I was no good for her when I had planned on spending the rest of my life with her.

At the time, I felt like I was wearing a scarlet letter, that no one would want to hire me after being fired, that I must be a horrible employee. On top of that, how could I go to any other startup after I had already been at the best one? Surprisingly, working at Facebook, even for that brief period of time, has been one of the strongest things people mention about me, and has been a blessing, regardless of whether or not I got a huge payout. People know I worked there; they generally don't ask what happened and assume I'm good because of the caliber of talent in that company is known to be amazing. I'd like to think I'm pretty darn special myself :)

Sometimes I see the possessions that my former co-workers have and I get jealous. Not gonna lie. But I realize I have all the things I want in my life and no more money or material things would improve that.

I re-read an interview Mark did with *Rolling Stone* some time back. He said, "I'm not trying to get as rich as possible. I could have sold Facebook a while ago and had more than enough money than I would have known what to do with."

Working with Mark and hearing that quote reminded me how he was all about doing something great and not just about making money. It's a healthy reminder to keep doing that and you'll get whatever success you define for yourself.

My biggest takeaway from my Facebook experience was that it forced me to take an honest look at myself. That's fucking hard.

Why was I embarrassed that I got fired?

In what kind of company will I succeed in the future?

What did I do wrong so I can improve for next time?

I will be forever grateful to Facebook for hiring me. I got to spend a year at one of the most influential companies in my lifetime. Having that experience — and having it on my résumé — changed my life.

It's that experience that enabled me to go on and create valuable enterprises of my own:

→ Mint.com's early marketing strategy
→ AppSumo.com
→ Monthly1k.com
→ and my newest child, SumoMe.com

Good Times at Facebook

Soleio, Aditya, and me at the Holiday Party

Mark and Priscilla at TheFacebook Party (before it was just Facebook)

The whole team celebrating our 5 millionth user

Good times.

Acknowledgements

What do you do when you want to thank everyone?

A few times I've been listed in the acknowledge section of books. A few times I hadn't but selfishly I thought I deserved it.

Ultimately I want to thank everyone who's believed and supported me. Especially in some of my darker days.

This book would NOT have been finished without the significant help of:

Marti Motogames for criticizing my grammar.
Tucker Max for being the real Tucker Max
JT Trollman for suffering through my first draft
Lindsey M for actually taking time to leave great feedback
Zach O for being more persistent & annoying than my mother.
Yael G; for stepping up w/ edits & her interest in 50% improvement

Mark 3: for firing me and the chance to
    experience more in life
Everyone at AppSumo aka My fat ass family. Love y'all
Johnny Lester letting me sleep on the couch for days of
Erin for helping w/ the design.

Chad Boyden for being the greatest partner ever. If only
    you were a woman
The Adam Gilbert for being one of the most solid
    person I know.
Scott Hurff for sparking my ass to finish the book!

(Your Name here)

To everyone else I didn't include, email me
Love @ OKdork.com and I'll add you here
                                    to OKdork.com/love
Rabbit

Jonh/

What do you do when you want to thank everyone?

A few times I've been listed in the acknowledgements section of books. A few times I haven't but selfishly I thought I deserved it.

Ultimately, I want to thank everyone who's believed and supported me. Especially in some of my darker days.

This book would NOT have been finished without the significant help of:

→ *Marti Motoyama for criticizing my grammar*
→ *Tucker Max for being the real Tucker Max*
→ *JT Trollman for suffering through my first draft*
→ *Lindsey M. for actually taking time to leave great feedback*
→ *Zach O. for being more persistent and annoying than my mother*
→ *Yael G. for stepping up with edits and her interest in self improvement*
→ *Mark Z. for firing me and the chance to experience more in life*
→ *Everyone at AppSumo (a.k.a my fat ass family): love y'all*
→ *Johny Li for letting me sleep on the couch the day of*
→ *Erin for helping with the design*
→ *Chad Boyda for being the greatest partner ever (if only you were a woman)*
→ *Adam Gilbert for being one of the most solid people I know*
→ *Scott Herff for spanking my ass to finish the book!*
→ *[Your Name Here]*

To everyone else I didn't include, email me at love@okdork.com and I'll add you to okdork.com/love :)

<3 Noah

Want more great stories, marketing tools, and business hacks?

»»» OKDORK.COM/TACOS

You'll learn exactly how I started 2 multi-million dollar businesses, grew a 700,000+ email list, and where to find the best tacos in the world.

Made in the USA
Lexington, KY
15 September 2016